CONFIGURING PRODUCT INFORMATION MANAGEMENT WITHIN DYNAMICS 365 FOR FINANCE & OPERATIONS

MODULE 5: **CONFIGURING PRODUCT RELATIONSHIPS**

MURRAY FIFE

ISBN-13: 978-1078122887

Preface

What You Need for this Guide

All the examples shown in this blueprint were done with the Microsoft Dynamics 365 for Operations hosted image that was provisioned through Lifecycle Services.

The following list of software from the virtual image was leveraged within this guide:

Microsoft Dynamics 365 for Operations

Even though all the preceding software was used during the development and testing of the recipes in this book, they should also work on later versions without any changes.

Errata

Although we have taken every care to ensure the accuracy of our content, mistakes do happen. If you find a mistake in one of our books—may be a mistake in the text or the code—we would be grateful if you would report this to us. By doing so, you can save other readers from frustration and help us improve subsequent versions of this book. If you find any errata, please report them by emailing editor@dynamicscompanions.com.

Piracy

Piracy of copyright material on the Internet is an ongoing problem across all media. If you come across any illegal copies of our works, in any form, on the Internet, please provide us with the location address or website name immediately so that we can pursue a remedy.

Please contact us at legal@dynamicscompanions.com with a link to the suspected pirated material.

We appreciate your help in protecting our authors and our ability to bring you valuable content.

Questions

You can contact us at help@dynamicscompanions.com if you are having a problem with any aspect of the book, and we will do our best to address it.

Table of Contents

DYNAMICS COMPANIONS
BARE BONES CONFIGURATION GUIDE

CONFIGURING PRODUCT INFORMATION MANAGEMENT WITHIN DYNAMICS 365 FOR FINANCE & OPERATIONS
MODULE 5: CONFIGURING PRODUCT RELATIONSHIPS

Configuring Product Relationships

Another feature within the Product Information Management area that you may want to configure is the **Product Relationships** function. This allows you to create links between products to indicate that products are sold together, are alternate products, are commonly purchased together, or really anything that you like.

Topics Covered

- Configuring Product Relationship Types

- Review

dyn c
www.dynamicscompanions.com
Dynamics Companions

- 7 -

www.blindsquirrelpublishing.com
© 2017 Blind Squirrel Publishing, LLC , All Rights Reserved

BLIND SQUIRREL
PUBLISHING

DYNAMICS COMPANIONS
BARE BONES CONFIGURATION GUIDE

CONFIGURING PRODUCT INFORMATION MANAGEMENT WITHIN DYNAMICS 365 FOR FINANCE & OPERATIONS
MODULE 5: CONFIGURING PRODUCT RELATIONSHIPS

Configuring Product Relationship Types

The first step is to set up the different **Product Relationship Types** that you want to track.

Topics Covered

- Opening the Product relationship types form
- Creating a Customers also bought relationship
- Creating an Accessories relationship
- Creating a Frequently bought together relationship
- Creating an Alternative product relationship
- Creating a Spare parts relationship
- Creating an Upsell relationship
- Configuring Product Relationships
- Summary

www.dynamicscompanions.com
Dynamics Companions

- 8 -

www.blindsquirrelpublishing.com
© 2017 Blind Squirrel Publishing, LLC , All Rights Reserved

BLIND SQUIRREL
PUBLISHING

DYNAMICS COMPANIONS
BARE BONES CONFIGURATION GUIDE

CONFIGURING PRODUCT INFORMATION MANAGEMENT WITHIN DYNAMICS 365 FOR FINANCE & OPERATIONS
MODULE 5: CONFIGURING PRODUCT RELATIONSHIPS

Opening the Product relationship types form

Now we will want to create some relationships between the products.

To do this we will want to open the **Product relationship types** maintenance form which will allow us to link products together.

How to do it...

Step 1: Open the Product relationship types form through the menu

We can get to the **Product relationship types** form a couple of different ways. The first way is through the master menu.

Navigate to Product information management > Setup > Product relationship types.

Step 2: Open the Product relationship types form through the menu search

Another way that we can find the **Product relationship types** form is through the menu search feature.

Type in **product relat** into the menu search and select **Product relationship types**.

This will open up the **Product relationship types** maintenance form where we will be able to create different types of link options between products.

DYNAMICS COMPANIONS
BARE BONES CONFIGURATION GUIDE

CONFIGURING PRODUCT INFORMATION MANAGEMENT WITHIN DYNAMICS 365 FOR FINANCE & OPERATIONS
MODULE 5: CONFIGURING PRODUCT RELATIONSHIPS

Opening the Product relationship types form

How to do it...

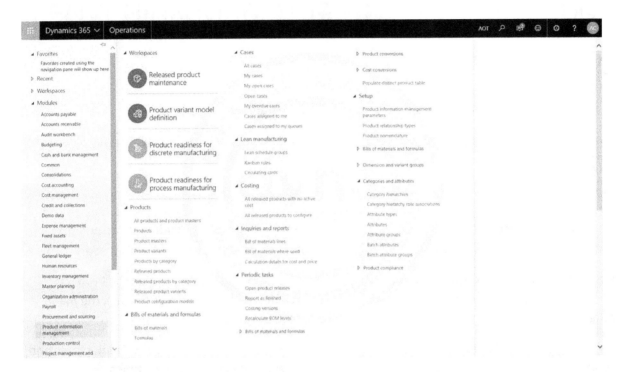

Step 1: Open the Product relationship types form through the menu

We can get to the **Product relationship types** form a couple of different ways. The first way is through the master menu.

To do this, open up the navigation panel, expand out the **Modules** and group, and click on **Product information management** to see all of the menu items that are available. Then click on the **Product relationship types** menu item within the **Setup** group.

dyn c
www.dynamicscompanions.com
Dynamics Companions

- 10 -

www.blindsquirrelpublishing.com
© 2017 Blind Squirrel Publishing, LLC , All Rights Reserved

BLIND SQUIRREL
PUBLISHING

DYNAMICS COMPANIONS
BARE BONES CONFIGURATION GUIDE

CONFIGURING PRODUCT INFORMATION MANAGEMENT WITHIN DYNAMICS 365 FOR FINANCE & OPERATIONS
MODULE 5: CONFIGURING PRODUCT RELATIONSHIPS

Opening the Product relationship types form

How to do it...

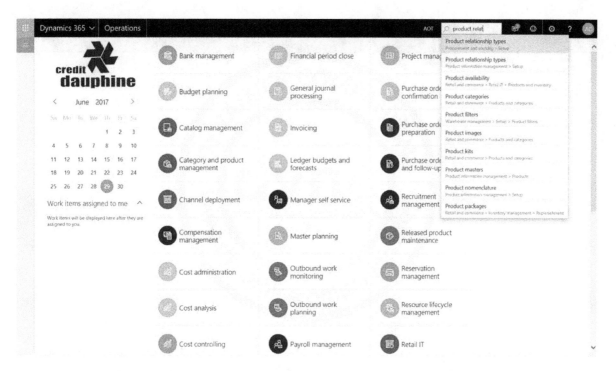

Step 2: Open the Product relationship types form through the menu search

Another way that we can find the **Product relationship types** form is through the menu search feature.

We can do this by clicking on the search icon in the header of the form (or by pressing **ALT+G**) and then type in **product relat** storage into the search box. Then you will be able to select the **Product relationship types** form from the dropdown list.

www.dynamicscompanions.com
Dynamics Companions

- 11 -

www.blindsquirrelpublishing.com
© 2017 Blind Squirrel Publishing, LLC , All Rights Reserved

BLIND SQUIRREL
PUBLISHING

DYNAMICS COMPANIONS
BARE BONES CONFIGURATION GUIDE

CONFIGURING PRODUCT INFORMATION MANAGEMENT WITHIN DYNAMICS 365 FOR FINANCE & OPERATIONS
MODULE 5: CONFIGURING PRODUCT RELATIONSHIPS

Opening the Product relationship types form

How to do it...

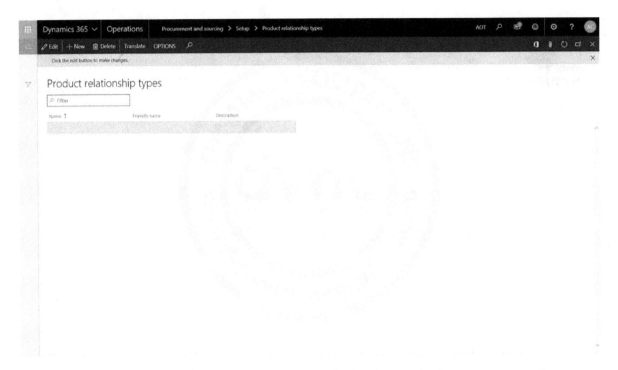

Step 2: Open the Product relationship types form through the menu search

This will open up the **Product relationship types** maintenance form where we will be able to create different types of link options between products.

dyn c
Dynamics companions

www.dynamicscompanions.com
Dynamics Companions

- 12 -

www.blindsquirrelpublishing.com
© 2017 Blind Squirrel Publishing, LLC , All Rights Reserved

BLIND SQUIRREL
PUBLISHING

DYNAMICS COMPANIONS
BARE BONES CONFIGURATION GUIDE

CONFIGURING PRODUCT INFORMATION MANAGEMENT WITHIN DYNAMICS 365 FOR FINANCE & OPERATIONS
MODULE 5: CONFIGURING PRODUCT RELATIONSHIPS

Creating a Customers also bought relationship

Now let's create a product relationship that allows us to specify that customers also bought other products when they purchased an particular product.

How to do it...

Step 1: Click New

We will start off by creating a new relationship type record.

Click on the **New** button.

Step 2: Update the Name

Now we will want to give our relationship a name for reference.

Set the Name to CustomersAlsoBought.

Step 3: Update the Friendly name

Next we will want to give the relationship a friendlier name.

Set the Friendly name to Customers also bought.

Step 4: Update the Description

And finally we will add a more detailed description for the relationship type.

Set the Description to Customers Who Bought This Also Bought These.

 www.dynamicscompanions.com
Dynamics Companions

- 13 -

www.blindsquirrelpublishing.com
© 2017 Blind Squirrel Publishing, LLC , All Rights Reserved

BLIND SQUIRREL
PUBLISHING

DYNAMICS COMPANIONS
BARE BONES CONFIGURATION GUIDE

CONFIGURING PRODUCT INFORMATION MANAGEMENT WITHIN DYNAMICS 365 FOR FINANCE & OPERATIONS
MODULE 5: CONFIGURING PRODUCT RELATIONSHIPS

Creating a Customers also bought relationship

How to do it...

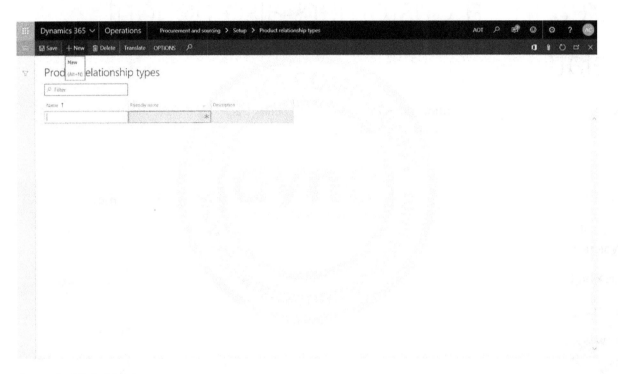

Step 1: Click New

We will start off by creating a new relationship type record.

To do this just click on the **New** button.

dync
dynamics companions
www.dynamicscompanions.com
Dynamics Companions

- 14 -

www.blindsquirrelpublishing.com
© 2017 Blind Squirrel Publishing, LLC , All Rights Reserved

BLIND SQUIRREL
PUBLISHING

DYNAMICS COMPANIONS
BARE BONES CONFIGURATION GUIDE

CONFIGURING PRODUCT INFORMATION MANAGEMENT WITHIN DYNAMICS 365 FOR FINANCE & OPERATIONS
MODULE 5: CONFIGURING PRODUCT RELATIONSHIPS

Creating a Customers also bought relationship

How to do it...

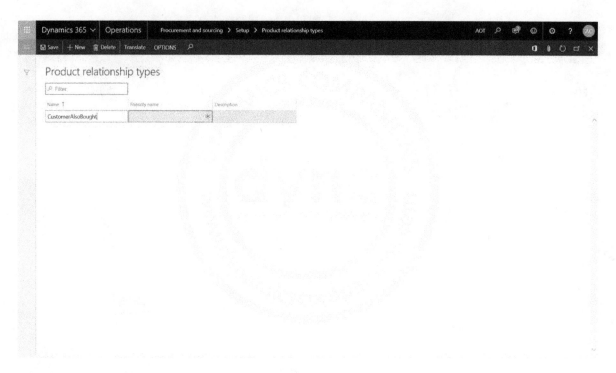

Step 2: Update the Name

Now we will want to give our relationship a name for reference.

To do this we will just need to update the **Name** value.

For this example, we will want to set the **Name** to **CustomersAlsoBought**.

dyn c

www.dynamicscompanions.com
Dynamics Companions

- 15 -

www.blindsquirrelpublishing.com
© 2017 Blind Squirrel Publishing, LLC , All Rights Reserved

BLIND SQUIRREL
PUBLISHING

DYNAMICS COMPANIONS
BARE BONES CONFIGURATION GUIDE

CONFIGURING PRODUCT INFORMATION MANAGEMENT WITHIN DYNAMICS 365 FOR FINANCE & OPERATIONS
MODULE 5: CONFIGURING PRODUCT RELATIONSHIPS

Creating a Customers also bought relationship

How to do it...

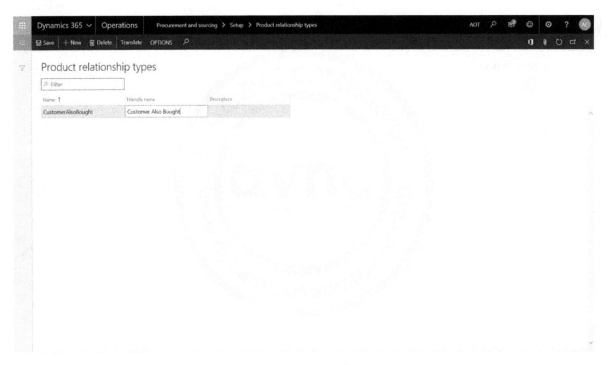

Step 3: Update the Friendly name

Next we will want to give the relationship a friendlier name.

To do this we will just need to update the **Friendly name** value.

For this example, we will want to set the **Friendly name** to **Customers also bought**.

dync
dynamics companion

www.dynamicscompanions.com
Dynamics Companions

- 16 -

www.blindsquirrelpublishing.com
© 2017 Blind Squirrel Publishing, LLC , All Rights Reserved

BLIND SQUIRREL
PUBLISHING

DYNAMICS COMPANIONS
BARE BONES CONFIGURATION GUIDE

CONFIGURING PRODUCT INFORMATION MANAGEMENT WITHIN DYNAMICS 365 FOR FINANCE & OPERATIONS
MODULE 5: CONFIGURING PRODUCT RELATIONSHIPS

Creating a Customers also bought relationship

How to do it...

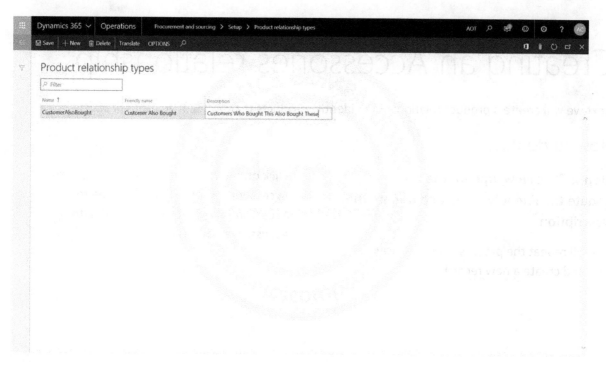

Step 4: Update the Description

And finally we will add a more detailed description for the relationship type.

To do this we will just need to update the **Description** value.

For this example, we will want to set the Description to Customers Who Bought This Also Bought These.

www.dynamicscompanions.com
Dynamics Companions

- 17 -

www.blindsquirrelpublishing.com
© 2017 Blind Squirrel Publishing, LLC, All Rights Reserved

BLIND SQUIRREL
PUBLISHING

DYNAMICS COMPANIONS
BARE BONES CONFIGURATION GUIDE

CONFIGURING PRODUCT INFORMATION MANAGEMENT WITHIN DYNAMICS 365 FOR FINANCE & OPERATIONS
MODULE 5: CONFIGURING PRODUCT RELATIONSHIPS

Creating an Accessories relationship

Next we will create a product relationship to identify products that accessorize other products.

How to do it...

Step 1: Click New, update the Name, update the Friendly name and update the Description

We will repeat the process from the previous step and create a new record.

Click on the New button, set the Name to Accessories, set the Friendly name to Accessories and set the Description to Accessories for this product.

dyn c
www.dynamicscompanions.com
Dynamics Companions

- 18 -

www.blindsquirrelpublishing.com
© 2017 Blind Squirrel Publishing, LLC, All Rights Reserved

 BLIND SQUIRREL PUBLISHING

DYNAMICS COMPANIONS
BARE BONES CONFIGURATION GUIDE

CONFIGURING PRODUCT INFORMATION MANAGEMENT WITHIN DYNAMICS 365 FOR FINANCE & OPERATIONS
MODULE 5: CONFIGURING PRODUCT RELATIONSHIPS

Creating an Accessories relationship

How to do it...

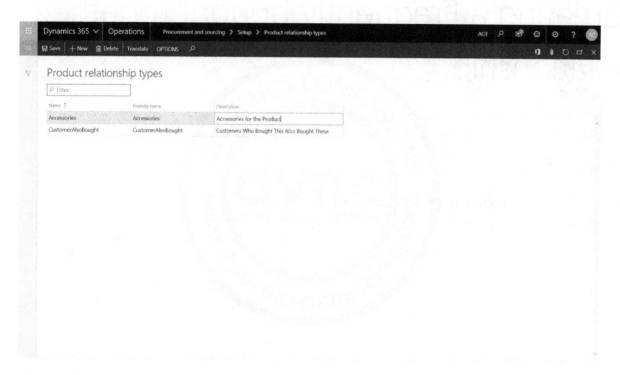

Step 1: Click New, update the Name, update the Friendly name and update the Description

We will repeat the process from the previous step and create a new record.

To do this just click on the **New** button, update the **Name** value, update the **Friendly name** value and update the **Description** value.

For this example, we will want to set the **Name** to **Accessories**, set the **Friendly name** to **Accessories** and set the **Description** to **Accessories for this product**.

dyn
www.dynamicscompanions.com
Dynamics Companions

- 19 -

www.blindsquirrelpublishing.com
© 2017 Blind Squirrel Publishing, LLC , All Rights Reserved

BLIND SQUIRREL
PUBLISHING

DYNAMICS COMPANIONS
BARE BONES CONFIGURATION GUIDE

CONFIGURING PRODUCT INFORMATION MANAGEMENT WITHIN DYNAMICS 365 FOR FINANCE & OPERATIONS
MODULE 5: CONFIGURING PRODUCT RELATIONSHIPS

Creating a Frequently bought together relationship

We will add another relationship type, and this one will be to identify products that are commonly purchased together, maybe as bundles of products.

How to do it...

Step 1: Click New, update the Name and update the Friendly name

Let's create a new relationship type record.

Click on the New button, set the Name to FrequentlyBoughtTogether and set the Friendly name to FrequentlyBoughtTogether > These Products are frequently bought together.

dync
www.dynamicscompanions.com
Dynamics Companions

- 20 -

www.blindsquirrelpublishing.com
© 2017 Blind Squirrel Publishing, LLC , All Rights Reserved

BLIND SQUIRREL
PUBLISHING

DYNAMICS COMPANIONS
BARE BONES CONFIGURATION GUIDE

CONFIGURING PRODUCT INFORMATION MANAGEMENT WITHIN DYNAMICS 365 FOR FINANCE & OPERATIONS
MODULE 5: CONFIGURING PRODUCT RELATIONSHIPS

Creating a Frequently bought together relationship

How to do it...

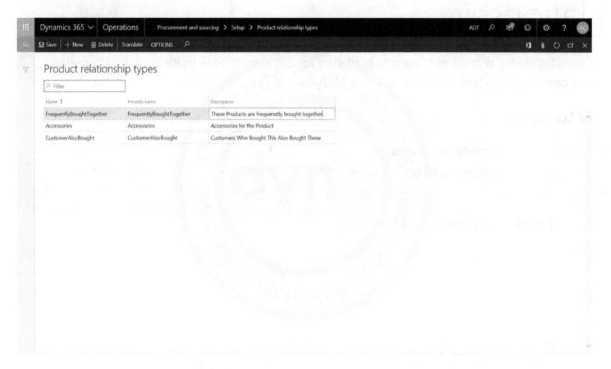

Step 1: Click New, update the Name and update the Friendly name

Let's create a new relationship type record.

To do this just click on the **New** button, update the **Name** value and update the **Friendly name** value.

For this example, we will want to set the Name to FrequentlyBoughtTogether and set the Friendly name to FrequentlyBoughtTogether > These Products are frequently bought together.

dync
www.dynamicscompanions.com
Dynamics Companions

- 21 -

www.blindsquirrelpublishing.com
© 2017 Blind Squirrel Publishing, LLC , All Rights Reserved

BLIND SQUIRREL
PUBLISHING

DYNAMICS COMPANIONS
BARE BONES CONFIGURATION GUIDE

CONFIGURING PRODUCT INFORMATION MANAGEMENT WITHIN DYNAMICS 365 FOR FINANCE & OPERATIONS
MODULE 5: CONFIGURING PRODUCT RELATIONSHIPS

Creating an Alternative product relationship

Another relationship that we may want to configure for our products are to identify the alternative product options just in case we don't have any of the original product in stock.

How to do it...

Step 1: Click New, update the Name, update the Friendly name and update the Description

All we need to do here is create another record.

Click on the New button, set the Name to Alternatives, set the Friendly name to AlternativeProducts and set the Description to These products are alternatives to this product.

dync
dynamics companions

www.dynamicscompanions.com
Dynamics Companions

- 22 -

www.blindsquirrelpublishing.com
© 2017 Blind Squirrel Publishing, LLC , All Rights Reserved

BLIND SQUIRREL
PUBLISHING

DYNAMICS COMPANIONS
BARE BONES CONFIGURATION GUIDE

CONFIGURING PRODUCT INFORMATION MANAGEMENT WITHIN DYNAMICS 365 FOR FINANCE & OPERATIONS
MODULE 5: CONFIGURING PRODUCT RELATIONSHIPS

Creating an Alternative product relationship

How to do it...

Step 1: Click New, update the Name, update the Friendly name and update the Description

All we need to do here is create another record.

To do this just click on the **New** button, update the **Name** value, update the **Friendly name** value and update the **Description** value.

For this example, we will want to set the Name to Alternatives, set the Friendly name to AlternativeProducts and set the Description to These products are alternatives to this product.

www.dynamicscompanions.com
Dynamics Companions

- 23 -

www.blindsquirrelpublishing.com
© 2017 Blind Squirrel Publishing, LLC , All Rights Reserved

BLIND SQUIRREL
PUBLISHING

DYNAMICS COMPANIONS
BARE BONES CONFIGURATION GUIDE

CONFIGURING PRODUCT INFORMATION MANAGEMENT WITHIN DYNAMICS 365 FOR FINANCE & OPERATIONS
MODULE 5: CONFIGURING PRODUCT RELATIONSHIPS

Creating a Spare parts relationship

If we have a product that we maintain spare parts or components for within the inventory then we may also want to have a relationship for that as well.

How to do it...

Step 1: Click New, update the Name, update the Friendly name and update the Description

Let's keep on creating new records for this type of relationship.

Click on the New button, set the Name to SpareParts, set the Friendly name to SpareParts and set the Description to These products are spare parts for this product.

dync
www.dynamicscompanions.com
Dynamics Companions

- 24 -

www.blindsquirrelpublishing.com
© 2017 Blind Squirrel Publishing, LLC, All Rights Reserved

BLIND SQUIRREL
PUBLISHING

DYNAMICS COMPANIONS
BARE BONES CONFIGURATION GUIDE

CONFIGURING PRODUCT INFORMATION MANAGEMENT WITHIN DYNAMICS 365 FOR FINANCE & OPERATIONS
MODULE 5: CONFIGURING PRODUCT RELATIONSHIPS

Creating a Spare parts relationship

How to do it...

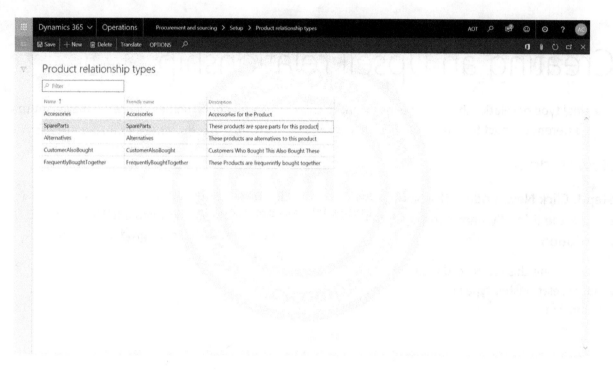

Step 1: Click New, update the Name, update the Friendly name and update the Description

Let's keep on creating new records for this type of relationship.

To do this just click on the **New** button, update the **Name** value, update the **Friendly name** value and update the **Description** value.

For this example, we will want to set the Name to SpareParts, set the Friendly name to SpareParts and set the Description to These products are spare parts for this product.

dync
www.dynamicscompanions.com
Dynamics Companions

- 25 -

www.blindsquirrelpublishing.com
© 2017 Blind Squirrel Publishing, LLC , All Rights Reserved

BLIND SQUIRREL
PUBLISHING

DYNAMICS COMPANIONS
BARE BONES CONFIGURATION GUIDE

CONFIGURING PRODUCT INFORMATION MANAGEMENT WITHIN DYNAMICS 365 FOR FINANCE & OPERATIONS
MODULE 5: CONFIGURING PRODUCT RELATIONSHIPS

Creating an Upsell relationship

One final type of relationship that we may want to track are upsell opportunities where we may want to sell a different product than the one that the customer is ordering.

How to do it...

Step 1: Click New, update the Name, update the Friendly name and update the Description

We will create this last record within the **Product relationship types** form for this type of relationship.

Click on the New button, set the Name to Upsell, set the Friendly name to Upsell and set the Description to These products may be upsold.

dync
www.dynamicscompanions.com
Dynamics Companions

- 26 -

www.blindsquirrelpublishing.com
© 2017 Blind Squirrel Publishing, LLC, All Rights Reserved

BLIND SQUIRREL
PUBLISHING

DYNAMICS COMPANIONS
BARE BONES CONFIGURATION GUIDE

CONFIGURING PRODUCT INFORMATION MANAGEMENT WITHIN DYNAMICS 365 FOR FINANCE & OPERATIONS
MODULE 5: CONFIGURING PRODUCT RELATIONSHIPS

Creating an Upsell relationship

How to do it...

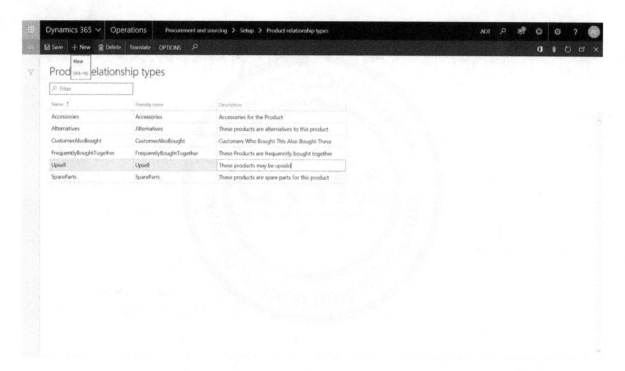

Step 1: Click New, update the Name, update the Friendly name and update the Description

We will create this last record within the **Product relationship types** form for this type of relationship.

To do this just click on the **New** button, update the **Name** value, update the **Friendly name** value and update the **Description** value.

For this example, we will want to set the **Name** to **Upsell**, set the **Friendly name** to **Upsell** and set the **Description** to **These products may be upsold**.

www.dynamicscompanions.com
Dynamics Companions

- 27 -

www.blindsquirrelpublishing.com
© 2017 Blind Squirrel Publishing, LLC , All Rights Reserved

BLIND SQUIRREL
PUBLISHING

DYNAMICS COMPANIONS
BARE BONES CONFIGURATION GUIDE

CONFIGURING PRODUCT INFORMATION MANAGEMENT WITHIN DYNAMICS 365 FOR FINANCE & OPERATIONS
MODULE 5: CONFIGURING PRODUCT RELATIONSHIPS

Configuring Product Relationships

Once you have defined the **Relationships** you can start using them within the **Released Products**.

How to do it...

Step 1: Open Released products and click Related products

Open up the **Released products** form, find the product and click on the **Related products** button.

This will open up the **Related Products** maintenance form where we will be able to link other products to the main record.

Step 2: Click New

We will want to now add a product record to the **Related products** list.

Click on the **New** button.

Step 3: Select the Product number

Once we have a new record we can search through the list of products and find the one that we want to link to the parent product.

Click on the **Product number** dropdown list and select **701400**.

Step 4: Update the Relationship type

And then we will want to specify the way that we want to relate the products together.

Set the Relationship type to SpareParts.

Step 5: Click New, update the Product number and update the Relationship type

We can continue adding more product relationships by repeating the process.

Click on the **New** button, set the **Product number** to **701600** and set the **Relationship type** to **SpareParts**.

Step 6: Click New, update the Product number and update the Relationship type

Also, we can create relationships of different types as well.

Click on the New button, set the Product number to 006R0175 and set the Relationship type to Accessories.

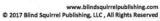

DYNAMICS COMPANIONS
BARE BONES CONFIGURATION GUIDE

CONFIGURING PRODUCT INFORMATION MANAGEMENT WITHIN DYNAMICS 365 FOR FINANCE & OPERATIONS
MODULE 5: CONFIGURING PRODUCT RELATIONSHIPS

Configuring Product Relationships

How to do it...

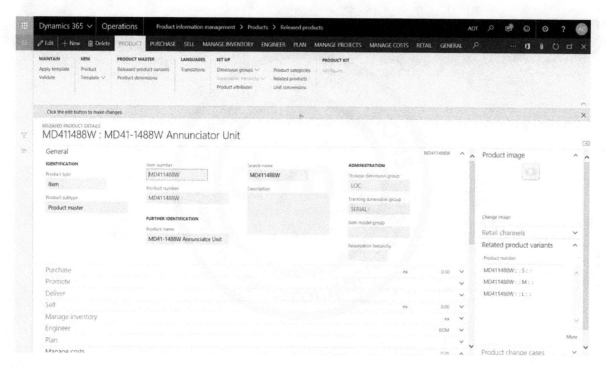

Step 1: Open Released products and click Related products

To do this just open up the **Released products** form and find the product that you want to maintain and click on the **Related products** button.

For this example we selected the **MD411488W** product.

dync
www.dynamicscompanions.com
Dynamics Companions

- 29 -

www.blindsquirrelpublishing.com
© 2017 Blind Squirrel Publishing, LLC , All Rights Reserved

BLIND SQUIRREL
PUBLISHING

DYNAMICS COMPANIONS
BARE BONES CONFIGURATION GUIDE

CONFIGURING PRODUCT INFORMATION MANAGEMENT WITHIN DYNAMICS 365 FOR FINANCE & OPERATIONS
MODULE 5: CONFIGURING PRODUCT RELATIONSHIPS

Configuring Product Relationships

How to do it...

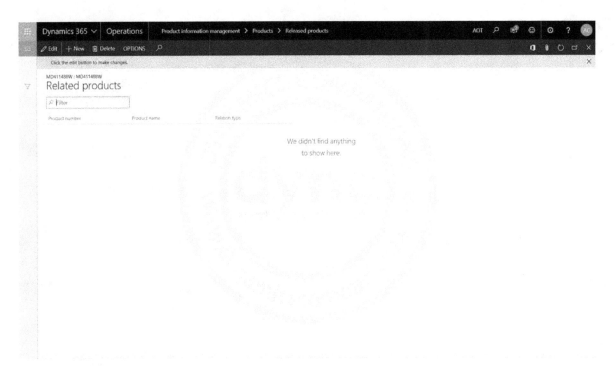

Step 1: Open Released products and click Related products

This will open up the **Related Products** maintenance form where we will be able to link other products to the main record.

www.dynamicscompanions.com
Dynamics Companions

www.blindsquirrelpublishing.com
© 2017 Blind Squirrel Publishing, LLC , All Rights Reserved

BLIND SQUIRREL
PUBLISHING

DYNAMICS COMPANIONS
BARE BONES CONFIGURATION GUIDE

CONFIGURING PRODUCT INFORMATION MANAGEMENT WITHIN DYNAMICS 365 FOR FINANCE & OPERATIONS
MODULE 5: CONFIGURING PRODUCT RELATIONSHIPS

Configuring Product Relationships

How to do it...

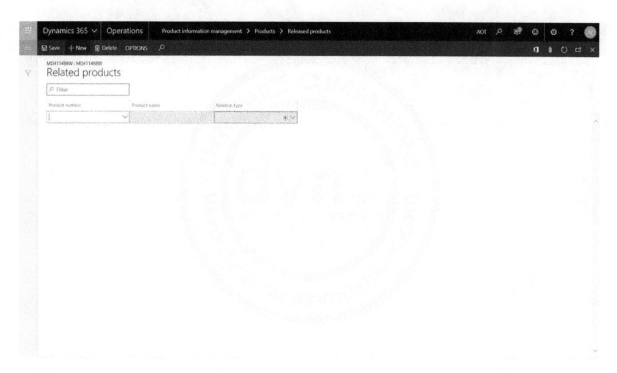

Step 2: Click New

We will want to now add a product record to the **Related products** list.

To do this just click on the **New** button.

www.dynamicscompanions.com
Dynamics Companions

- 31 -

www.blindsquirrelpublishing.com
© 2017 Blind Squirrel Publishing, LLC , All Rights Reserved

BLIND SQUIRREL
PUBLISHING

DYNAMICS COMPANIONS
BARE BONES CONFIGURATION GUIDE

CONFIGURING PRODUCT INFORMATION MANAGEMENT WITHIN DYNAMICS 365 FOR FINANCE & OPERATIONS
MODULE 5: CONFIGURING PRODUCT RELATIONSHIPS

Configuring Product Relationships

How to do it...

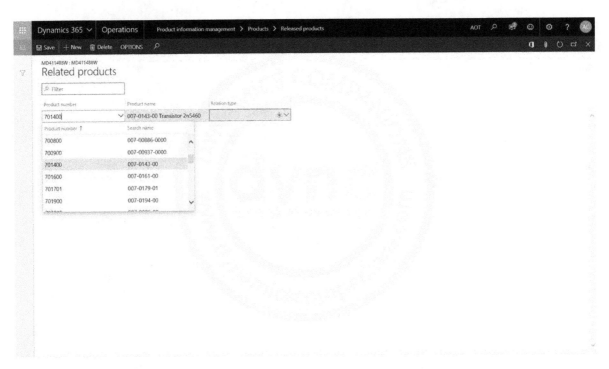

Step 3: Select the Product number

Once we have a new record we can search through the list of products and find the one that we want to link to the parent product.

To do this we will just need to select the **Product number** from the dropdown list.

For this example, we will want to click on the **Product number** dropdown list and select **701400**.

dyn c
dynamics companions
www.dynamicscompanions.com
Dynamics Companions

- 32 -

www.blindsquirrelpublishing.com
© 2017 Blind Squirrel Publishing, LLC, All Rights Reserved

BLIND SQUIRREL
PUBLISHING

DYNAMICS COMPANIONS
BARE BONES CONFIGURATION GUIDE

CONFIGURING PRODUCT INFORMATION MANAGEMENT WITHIN DYNAMICS 365 FOR FINANCE & OPERATIONS
MODULE 5: CONFIGURING PRODUCT RELATIONSHIPS

Configuring Product Relationships

How to do it...

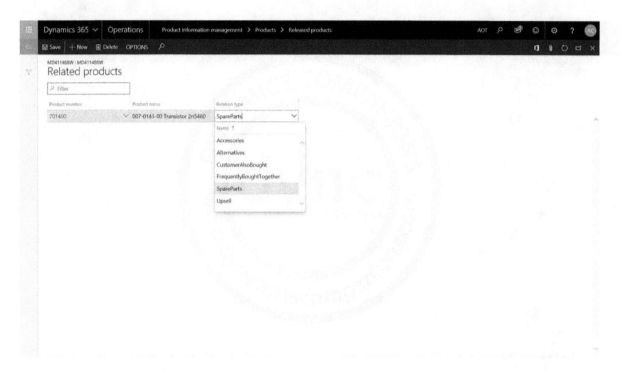

Step 4: Update the Relationship type

And then we will want to specify the way that we want to relate the products together.

To do this we will just need to update the **Relationship type** value.

For this example, we will want to set the **Relationship type** to **SpareParts**.

DYNAMICS COMPANIONS
BARE BONES CONFIGURATION GUIDE

CONFIGURING PRODUCT INFORMATION MANAGEMENT WITHIN DYNAMICS 365 FOR FINANCE & OPERATIONS
MODULE 5: CONFIGURING PRODUCT RELATIONSHIPS

Configuring Product Relationships

How to do it...

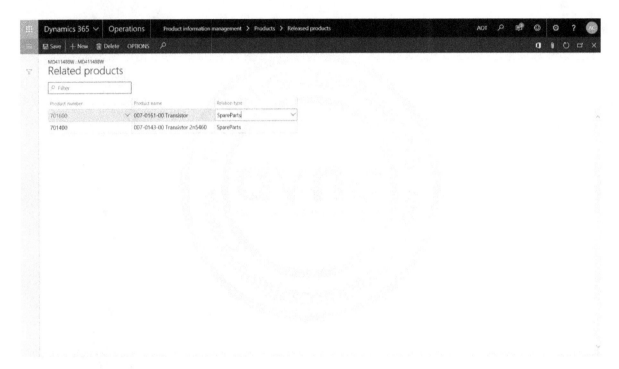

Step 5: Click New, update the Product number and update the Relationship type

We can continue adding more product relationships by repeating the process.

To do this just click on the **New** button, update the **Product number** value and update the **Relationship type** value.

For this example, we will want to set the **Product number** to **701600** and set the **Relationship type** to **SpareParts**.

dync
www.dynamicscompanions.com
Dynamics Companions

- 34 -

www.blindsquirrelpublishing.com
© 2017 Blind Squirrel Publishing, LLC, All Rights Reserved

BLIND SQUIRREL
PUBLISHING

DYNAMICS COMPANIONS
BARE BONES CONFIGURATION GUIDE

CONFIGURING PRODUCT INFORMATION MANAGEMENT WITHIN DYNAMICS 365 FOR FINANCE & OPERATIONS
MODULE 5: CONFIGURING PRODUCT RELATIONSHIPS

Configuring Product Relationships

How to do it...

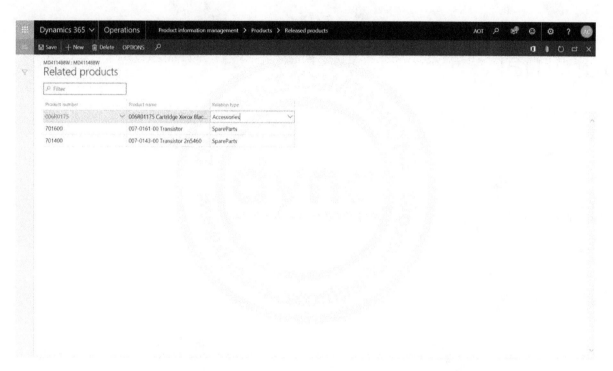

Step 6: Click New, update the Product number and update the Relationship type

Also, we can create relationships of different types as well.

To do this just click on the **New** button, update the **Product number** value and update the **Relationship type** value.

For this example, we will want to set the **Product number** to **006R0175** and set the **Relationship type** to **Accessories**.

dyn c
www.dynamicscompanions.com
Dynamics Companions

- 35 -

www.blindsquirrelpublishing.com
© 2017 Blind Squirrel Publishing, LLC , All Rights Reserved

BLIND SQUIRREL
PUBLISHING

DYNAMICS COMPANIONS
BARE BONES CONFIGURATION GUIDE

CONFIGURING PRODUCT INFORMATION MANAGEMENT WITHIN DYNAMICS 365 FOR FINANCE & OPERATIONS
MODULE 5: CONFIGURING PRODUCT RELATIONSHIPS

Summary

That was too easy.

www.dynamicscompanions.com
Dynamics Companions

- 36 -

www.blindsquirrelpublishing.com
© 2017 Blind Squirrel Publishing, LLC, All Rights Reserved

BLIND SQUIRREL
PUBLISHING

DYNAMICS COMPANIONS
BARE BONES CONFIGURATION GUIDE

CONFIGURING PRODUCT INFORMATION MANAGEMENT WITHIN DYNAMICS 365 FOR FINANCE & OPERATIONS
MODULE 5: CONFIGURING PRODUCT RELATIONSHIPS

Review

In this section we set up some of the softer (and looser) relationships between the products. By using the **Product Relationships** we can create different types of links between the products that we can use for reporting, and also just for lookups within the system.

www.dynamicscompanions.com
Dynamics Companions

- 37 -

www.blindsquirrelpublishing.com
© 2017 Blind Squirrel Publishing, LLC , All Rights Reserved

BLIND SQUIRREL
PUBLISHING

DYNAMICS COMPANIONS
BARE BONES CONFIGURATION GUIDE

CONFIGURING PRODUCT INFORMATION MANAGEMENT WITHIN DYNAMICS 365 FOR FINANCE & OPERATIONS
MODULE 5: CONFIGURING PRODUCT RELATIONSHIPS

About The Author

Murray Fife is an Author of over 20 books on Microsoft Dynamics including the Bare Bones Configuration Guide series. These guides comprise of over 15 books which step you through the setup and configuration of Microsoft Dynamics including Finance, Operations, Human Resources, Production, Service Management, and Project Accounting.

Throughout his 25+ years of experience in the software industry he has worked in many different roles during his career, including as a developer, an implementation consultant, a trainer and a demo guy within the partner channel which gives him a great understanding of the requirements for both customers and partners perspective.

If you are interested in contacting Murray or want to follow his blogs and posts then here is all of his contact information:

Email: murray@murrayfife.com

Twitter: @murrayfife
Facebook: facebook.com/murraycfife
Google: google.com/+murrayfife
LinkedIn: linkedin.com/in/murrayfife

Blog: atinkerersnotebook.com
Slideshare: slideshare.net/murrayfife
Amazon: amazon.com/author/murrayfife

DYNAMICS COMPANIONS
BARE BONES CONFIGURATION GUIDE

CONFIGURING PRODUCT INFORMATION MANAGEMENT WITHIN DYNAMICS 365 FOR FINANCE & OPERATIONS
MODULE 5: CONFIGURING PRODUCT RELATIONSHIPS

Need More Help with Microsoft Dynamics AX 2012 or Dynamics 365 for Operations

We are firm believers that Microsoft Dynamics AX 2012 or Dynamics 365 is not a hard product to learn, but the problem is where do you start. Which is why we developed the Bare Bones Configuration Guides. The aim of this series is to step you though the configuration of Microsoft Dynamics from a blank system, and then step you through the setup of all of the core modules within Microsoft Dynamics. We start with the setup of a base system, then move on to the financial, distribution, and operations modules.

Each book builds upon the previous ones, and by the time you have worked through all of the guides then you will have completely configured a simple (but functional) Microsoft Dynamics instance. To make it even more worthwhile you will have a far better understanding of Microsoft Dynamics and also how everything fits together.

As of now there are 16 guides in this series broken out as follows:

- Configuring a Training Environment
- Configuring an Organization
- Configuring the General Ledger
- Configuring Cash and Bank Management
- Configuring Accounts Receivable
- Configuring Accounts Payable
- Configuring Product Information Management
- Configuring Inventory Management

- Configuring Procurement and Sourcing
- Configuring Sales Order Management
- Configuring Human Resource Management
- Configuring Project Management and Accounting
- Configuring Production Control
- Configuring Sales and Marketing
- Configuring Service Management
- Configuring Warehouse Management

Although you can get each of these guides individually, and we think that each one is a great Visual resources to step you through each of the particular modules, for those of you that want to take full advantage of the series, you will want to start from the beginning and work through them one by one. After you have done that you would have done people told me was impossible for one persons to do, and that is to configure all of the core modules within Microsoft Dynamics.

If you are interested in finding out more about the series and also view all of the details including topics covered within the module, then browse to the Bare Bones Configuration Guide landing page on the Microsoft Dynamics Companions website. You will find all of the details, and also downloadable resources that help you with the setup of Microsoft Dynamics. Here is the full link: http://www.dynamicscompanions.com/

www.dynamicscompanions.com
Dynamics Companions

- 41 -

www.blindsquirrelpublishing.com
© 2017 Blind Squirrel Publishing, LLC , All Rights Reserved

BLIND SQUIRREL
PUBLISHING